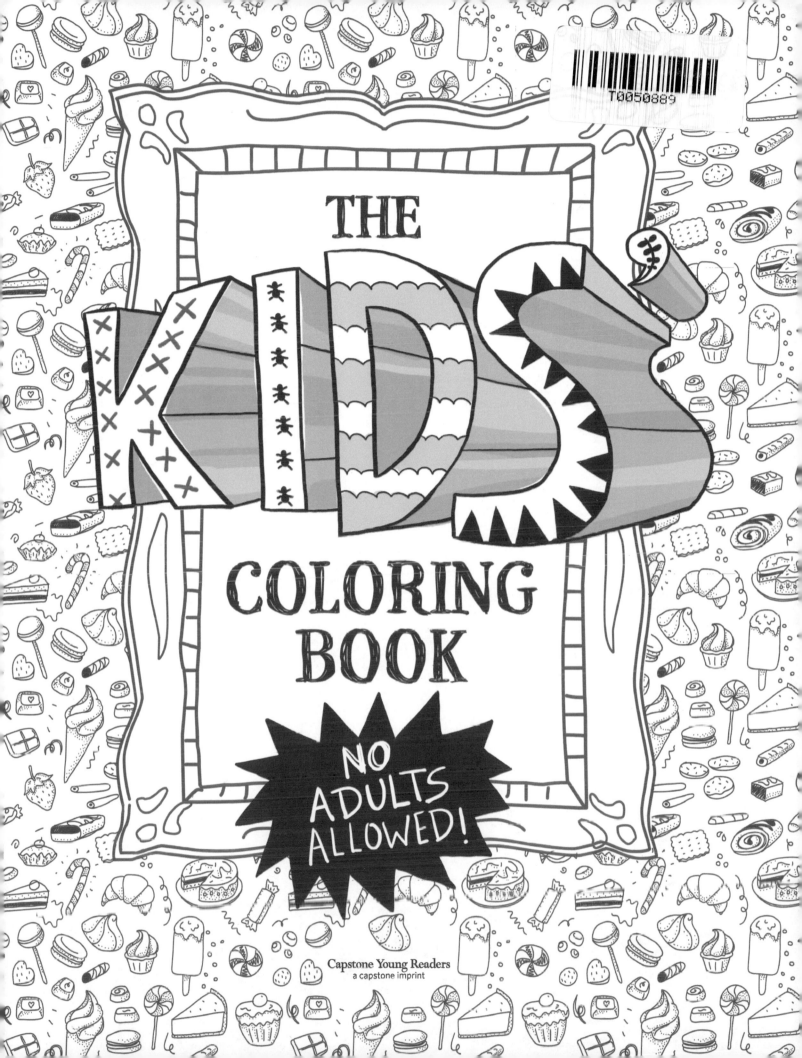

THE KIDS COLORING BOOK

NO ADULTS ALLOWED!

Capstone Young Readers
a capstone imprint

Published in 2017 by Capstone Young Readers,
A Capstone Imprint
1710 Roe Crest Drive, North Mankato, Minnesota 56003

www.mycapstone.com

Cataloging-in-Publication Data is available on the Library of Congress website.

ISBN: 978-1-62370-856-6 (paperback)

Designers: Aruna Rangarajan and Kay Fraser
Art Director: Heather Kindseth Wutschke
Media Researcher: Jo Miller
Production Specialist: Tori Abraham

Image Credits: Capstone: Bill McGuire, Bob Lentz, Cedric Hohnstadt, Daryll Collins, Dennis
Messner, Doug Holgate, Jess Bradley, Lucy Makuc, Steve Harpster; Shutterstock: 100ker, 9george,
Alex Rockheart, alfaori, alicedaniel, Anna Bogatirewa, Anna.zabella, Arisa_J, artenot, Artishok,
Art'nLera, artplay, AuraLux, Axro, balabolka, Bimbim, blackberry-jelly, blue67design, Brian Goff,
Brosko, Buchan, Cat Design, Cerama_ama, Chief Crow Daria, cornflower, Domenick, Drekhann,
fraulein_freya, FuzzylLogicKate, Gluiki, handiniatmodiwiryo, Ilya Zonov, ImHope, Incomible,
ingaart, Irina Adamovich, IrinaKrivoruchko, IvanNikulin, Julia Henze, Julia Snegireva,
Kalenik Hanna, Katerina Pereverzeva, KatiKapik, Kite-Kit, kzhu, Leona Kali, LHF Graphics,
lineartestpilot, liskus, Lychy, Magnia, Maryna S, merion_merion, Nadezhda Molkentin, Natalia
Chuen, Natalia Sheinkin, natsa, ngocdai86, nicemonkey, Nikolaeva, Nuarevik, Olga_Angelloz,
OlichO, Orfeev, pa3x, PAlartist, palform, panki, pzAxe, RetroClipArt, SunshienFlowers, svaga,
Teamarwen, tets, totallyjamie, UyUy, Val_Iva, Vanzyst, Vasilixa, Vecster, Vlad Young, Yana
Tomashova, YAZZIK, Yevhen Tamavskyi, Yuravector, zelena, zizar, zizi_mentos, zsooofija

Printed in the United States   5669

NAME:

_____

ARE YOU 18 YEARS OF AGE
OR YOUNGER?

☐ YES   ☐ NO

Signature: _____

Date: _____

*ATTENTION: By signing this legally binding and totally for reals contract, you confirm that you are under the age of 18. You are a legit, 100% real-life kid, who colors unabashedly for fun. You ARE NOT an adult. You do not color for the hobby's calming, stress-relieving, anti-anxiety benefits**, nor are you even aware that such benefits may or may not exist. Falsification of this document could result in a lifetime colored-pencil ban, mockery, or seriously bad karma.

**These statements have not been evaluated by the Food and Drug Administration, the United States Department of Agriculture, the Central Intelligence Agency, or the Global Society of Coloring. This product is not intended to diagnose, treat, or cure any disease, FYI (but hopefully you already knew that!).

Dear Adults,
STOP RIGHT THERE!! Put down the colored pencils, turn around, and walk away slowwwwly. This coloring book is NOT. FOR. YOU.

Dear Kids,
Phew! That was close.

As you may have noticed, adults have gone coloring-book crazy these days! They'll color anything within striking distance of their premium, ultra-fine markers: top-secret relaxation gardens, enchanted cat mandalas, calming kaleidoscopes, anti-stress sea animals, and other really, really boring stuff. (Really boring.)

But not this book! No siree! This book is JUST. FOR. YOU.

That's right, boys and girls. Introducing the first-ever adult coloring book for KIDS!

Bust out those old, waxy, broken crayons, and color inside the lines of these awesome illustrations for nothing other than plain-old primary fun! Or — *GASP!* — color OUTSIDE the lines! Who cares?! You're a kid, after all. Color like one.

Dear Adults,
If you're still reading this (and we know you are)...

KEEP OUT! BACK OFF! STAY AWAY!

This adult coloring book is

FOR KIDS ONLY!

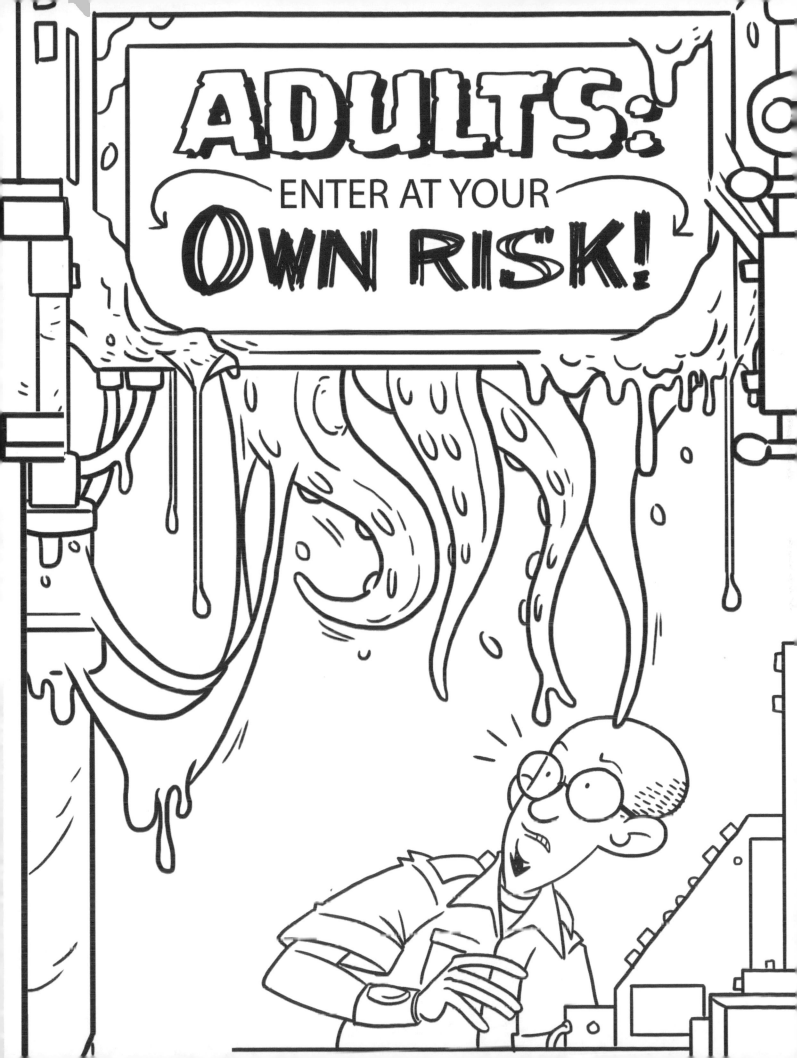

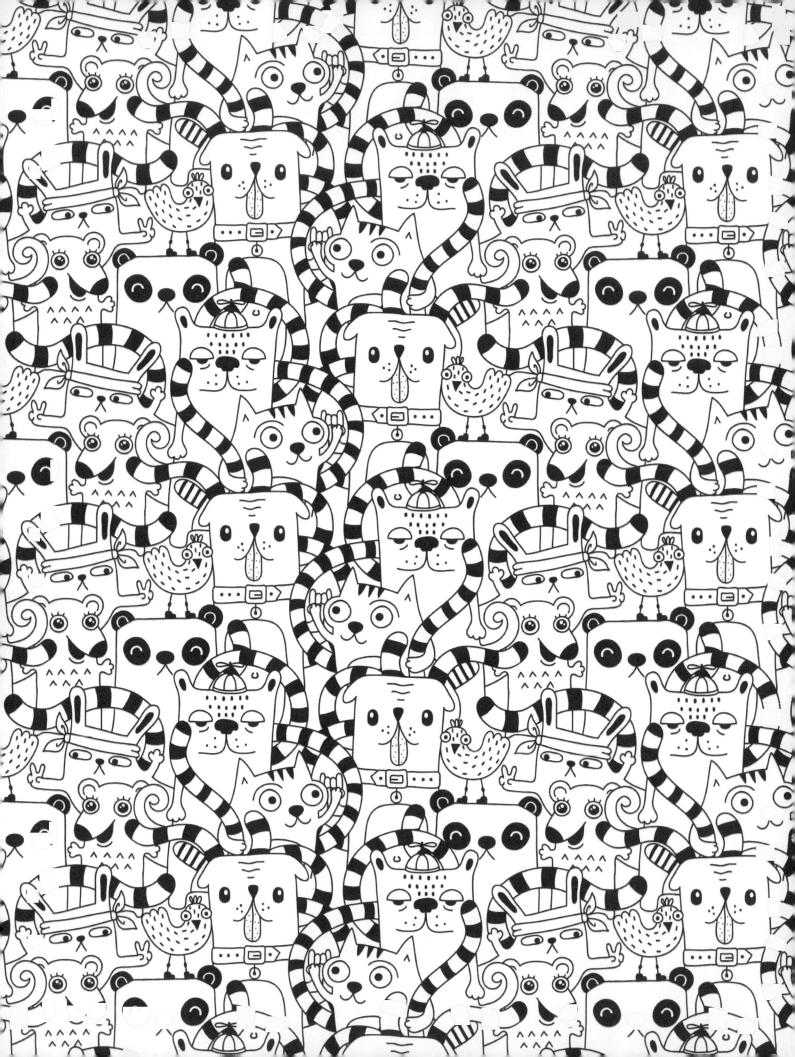

WHAT'S A MANDALA ANYWAY?

KEEP YOUR **TENTACLES** OFF MY COLORING BOOK!

FOR AGES

1 to 100

minus ages

18 to 99

NEVER
SAY
NEVER
(but NEVER color in
this book, Grandpa!)

COLOR INSIDE THE LINES.
—SAID SOMEONE WHO WAS WRONG

#kidstuff

P911! PARENT ALERT!

WHAT'S NEXT? VIDEO GAMES FOR ADULTS?

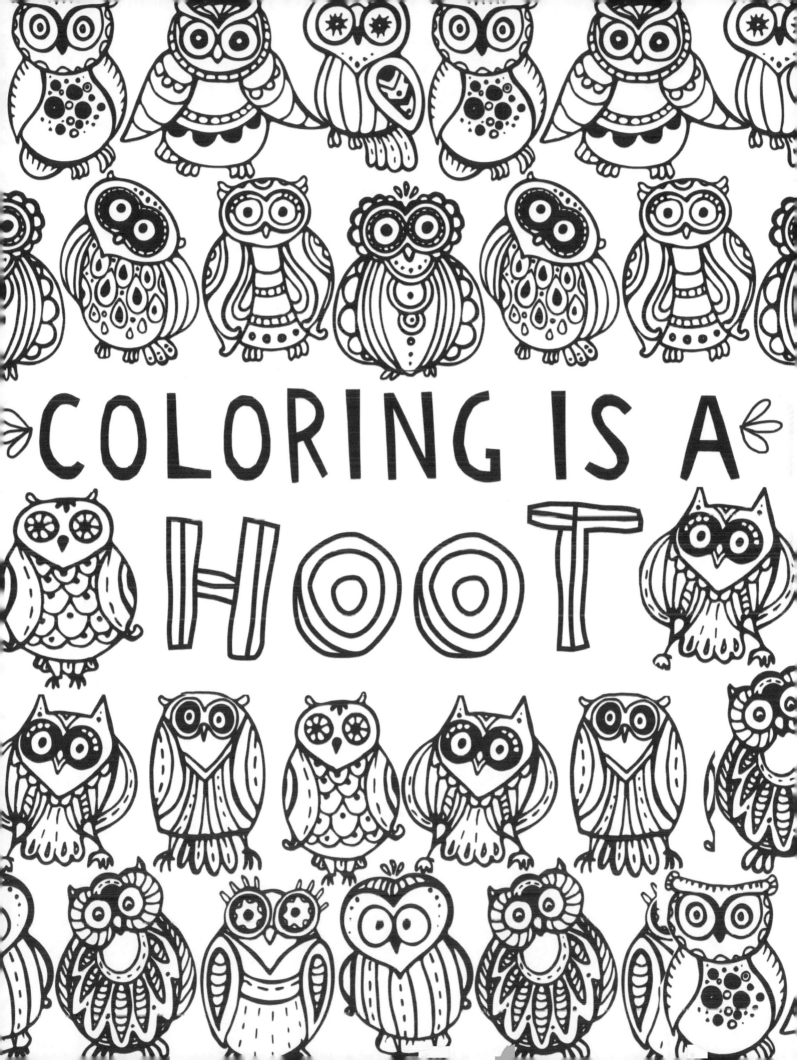

COLORING IS A HOOT

№ 0001

Certificate of achievement

This certificate is awarded to

for successfully proving that

*coloring isn't just for adults anymore!**

_____
President, Global Society of Coloring

_____
Date

*If you are an adult, consider this a Certificate of Failure, since you obviously didn't follow directions.